To my friend,
    William J. Fay,
with the esteem and
affection of
        John Tracy Ellis

Washington, D.C.
June 11, 1986

A Commitment to Truth

by

John Tracy Ellis

Wimmer Lecture XIX

The Archabbey Press
Latrobe, Pennsylvania

Library of Congress Cat. No. 66-18697

Nihil obstat: Francis J. Mueller
Deputatis ad hoc

Imprimatur: ✠Wm. G. Connare
Bishop of Greensburg
January 13, 1966

Wimmer Lecture XIX

Saint Vincent College

Latrobe, Pennsylvania

THE WIMMER LECTURE

In 1946, on the occasion of the centenary year of Saint Vincent Archabbey and College, the Board of Directors inaugurated the annual Wimmer Lecture in honor of Archabbot Boniface Wimmer. Since that time the series has attracted excellent scholars, among them Kenneth J. Conant, Erwin Panofsky, Gerald Phelan, Pitirim Sorokin, Jacques Maritain, Christopher Dawson, and Jean Ladriere.

Boniface Wimmer was the patriarch of American Benedictinism. He founded not only Saint Vincent but, directly or indirectly, is responsible for, and I am quite sure proud of, such institutions as St. John's Abbey and University in Minnesota, St. Benedict's Abbey and College in Kansas, St. Anselm's Abbey and College in New Hampshire, St. Mary's Abbey and College in New Jersey, Belmont Abbey and College in North Carolina, St. Bernard's Abbey and College in Alabama, St. Bede's Abbey and College in Peru, Illinois, St. Leo's Abbey and College in Florida.

In 1965 we were pleased and honored to have that distinguished scholar and champion of rights, John Tracy Ellis, for the Wimmer Lecture.

The brilliant manner in which he has distinguished himself is well known to all those knowledgeable in academe, church affairs, and all public matters. His statements have stirred our imagination, arousing the indignation of some while commanding the high respect of all.

The list of Monsignor Ellis's publications is impressive in its historical command and excellence. He is perhaps best known for his article of 1955 in which he questioned the intellectual life of the American Catholic. The article received a deserved response and eventually became highly influential in determining the direction of Catholic intellectuals or would-be intellectuals in the following years. It raised provocative, disturbing questions, but it also contributed one definitive answer, namely, that there are at least a few such genuine intellectuals on the American scene, one of whom is John Tracy Ellis himself.

The 1965 Wimmer Lecture will be a notable contribution to current ecumenical activity. It is beyond a doubt a landmark in the Wimmer Series. Because it catalogues some grave mistakes churchmen have made in the past, it is not always comfortable reading. Nevertheless, it is a constructive lecture, for it underlines in brilliant fashion how honest we have come to be. It is encouraging, too, because it points to a new future in the Christian Church. That future, even as the past, will undoubtedly disclose mistakes made by men who because they are men are not infallible. More importantly, that future will give us the fortitude to acknowledge our mistakes, the willingness to correct them, the open-mindedness to be all things to all men.

Father Maynard J. Brennan, O.S.B.
President Saint Vincent College

THREE WEEKS AFTER THE DEATH OF Pope John XXIII the ranking Protestant weekly of the United States, the *Christian Century*, published the following bit of verse:

> HISTORY, with its reversals,
> Cannot wreck this tomb.
> Here is no image to be disenthroned.
> Here is no myth to be destroyed.
> This life was too plain, too clear;
> Too many people saw the smiling truth
> For any future raid to steal such honor.
> No sentry need be posted,
> No watchman set to guard
> The tomb that is a hundred million hearts.[1]

In this simple poem Edith Lovejoy Pierce caught the authentic image of that extraordinary man whose reign of less than five years inaugurated a new era in the history of the people of God who constitute His Church. Were one asked to designate what it was that most clearly identified the aged pontiff in the mind and heart of the world, I should be inclined to say that it was his genius in demonstrating in his person the living reality of his repeated emphasis on the supreme value and healing quality of truth. In his first encyclical, *Ad Petri Cathedram*, of June, 1959, Pope John sounded this note in attributing the cause of humanity's discords and dissensions to what he called "ignorance of the truth, or what is worse, rejection of the truth once it has been sought and found."[2] The Christmas message of 1960 returned to the same theme in exhorting men to honor what was true. "It ennobles whoever professes it openly and without fear of others," said the pope. "Why, then, fear to honour it and make it respect-

Two

ed?" And then he added, "Not alone in guilt is he who deliberately obscures the truth; just as guilty is he who, from fear of not seeming complete and up-to-date, betrays it by the ambiguity of his attitude."[3]

It was the very lack of ambiguity in John XXIII's attitude toward others that explains in good measure the almost universal appeal he had for his contemporaries of every creed and race. The quality was revealed on countless occasions as, for example, when in addressing the representatives of the Eastern Churches early in the pontificate he expressed a desire for Christian reunion. He assured the Orthodox that he had not in mind to hold an historical trial to determine the cause of their unhappy differences since, as he said, his aim was not to point out who had been right and who had been wrong. "The responsibility," he remarked quite simply, "is shared on both sides."[4] The patent honesty and sincerity of these words were not lost on Christians of other communions who up to that time had been totally unaccustomed to hearing an admission of defect or error from the Church of Rome. Nor would it be an exaggeration to say that this approach brought almost at once a new and improved intellectual climate to the realm of interfaith and ecumenical endeavor.

Certainly the Holy Father did not lack strong scriptural warrant in his marked predilection for truthfulness and honesty in dealing with one's fellowmen. Thus when God dictated the commandments to Moses on Mount Sinai, there was no diminution of emphasis in the case of the commands, "Thou shalt not steal," and "Thou shalt not bear false witness against thy neighbor," as contrasted to the command, "Thou shalt not commit adultery."[5] And the New Testament gives even more striking evidence of Christ's admiration for forthrightness and honesty in human relationships, and His detestation of their opposites of pretense and deceit. For example, one of the most notable characteristics of Saint John the Baptist was his directness and his courageous defense of truth, even when that placed his personal interests in jeopardy. Not only was that the case in his public indictment of the illicit union between King Herod and the latter's sister-in-law;[6] it was the same when John's extraordinary apostolate at the Jordan River prompted some to believe him to be the long-awaited messiah. "You yourselves bear me witness," he insisted, "that I said 'I am not the Christ but have been sent before him,'" to which there was added the realistic

Five

reminder, "He must increase, but I must decrease."[7] It was conduct such as this that accounted in part for John's having won from the Son of God a tribute paid to no other man when Christ told His followers, "Amen I say to you, among those born of women there has not risen a greater than John the Baptist."[8]

To find that Christ should have set so high a premium on fidelity to honest speech and conduct comes as no surprise to anyone who has reflected on His life. From the outset of His public ministry our Lord's compassion for human weakness was apparent at every step. Thus did He turn aside the foolish ambition of James and John with a quiet remark concerning the price that must be paid for a place in His heavenly kingdom;[9] the adultery of the woman apprehended by the Scribes and Pharisees and brought before

Him in the temple, He readily forgave;[10] even the denial of Peter drew from Him nothing more than a saddened glance.[11] In no instance did Christ approve the defect, but since these actions were the consequence of human weakness, He was quick to bestow His pardon.

But it was quite otherwise when the Son of God was confronted with calculated insincerity and fraud. He made that plain in putting His disciples on guard against the Scribes and Pharisees, for, as He said,

> all their works they do in order to be seen by men; for they...love the first places at suppers and the front seats in the synagogues, and greetings in the market place, and to be called by men 'Rabbi.'[12]

If for nearly 2,000 years the heirs of the Christian tradition have found enchantment in the moral beauty of the eight beatitudes in the Sermon on the Mount, it should not be forgotten that at another time the same Voice, speaking directly to the Scribes and Pharisees, uttered eight maledictions which embody the most caustic condemnation of insincerity ever uttered. They were words which even at this distant time induce almost a shudder in one who recalls Who Christ was, and that He never said anything that He did not mean. On this occasion, turning on these masters of deceit, He exclaimed:

> Woe to you...hypocrites! because you are like whited sepulchres, which outwardly appear to men beautiful, but within are full of dead men's bones and of all uncleanness. So you also outwardly appear just to men, but within you are full of hypocrisy and iniquity.[13]

And at a later date in alluding to the punishment that would overtake the wicked servant, it seemed that our Lord could think of no sterner fate than to predict that the

Eight

master of such a one would "cut him asunder and make him share the lot of the hypocrites."[14]

Such, in brief, was Christ's teaching on matters relating to truthfulness and honesty, or to what is often described as character or personal integrity. Such, too, have been the principles that have inspired the teaching of the most authentic interpreters of the Christian way of life, as well as the personal actions of outstanding figures in the history of the Church whose lives were informed and governed by those principles. Dante, for example, reflected this in adopting the Aristotelian–Thomistic pattern in determining the hierarchy of suffering delineated in the 'Inferno' of his *Divine Comedy* where, as one writer has said, the reader finds that Dante "considers as the least the sins of incontinence, and as more serious those of violence, and still more serious those of fraud."[15] Obviously, there is no universal agreement as to precisely what constitutes character in a man, but in my judgment the distinguished English Benedictine historian, Dom David Knowles, summarized the necessary ingredients very satisfactorily some years ago in his inaugural lecture as Regius professor of modern history in the University of Cambridge. He spoke of the historian's difficulty in detecting and delineating the true characteristics of historical figures, and then he remarked:

> As he watches, he looks to see whether a man, by and large during his life, shows any evidence of acting according to a divine or moral law outside himself, whether he ever sacrifices his own profit or pleasure for the sake of a person or a principle; whether he shows evidence of loving other men, where by love we understand the classical definition of wishing

them well and doing well to them; whether
he puts justice before expediency; whether
he is sincere and truthful.[16]

Needless to say, no two men, whether
they be still alive or have passed into history,
will emerge with an identical image when
judged by these norms. For instance, great
in many ways though Saint Thomas Becket
undoubtedly was, in history's final reckoning
he is not likely to achieve the same degree
of moral grandeur that has gathered about
the names of those English saints of a later
time, John Fisher and Thomas More. In
Fisher and More discerning minds have
sensed the well nigh perfect fulfillment of the
ideal of human integrity. They manifested
it many times, but especially on such occasions as the day in 1535 that Henry VIII
sent a delegation of bishops to the Tower of
London to persuade Fisher to take the oath
demanded by the Act of Supremacy. Far

Eleven

from availing himself of this opportunity to regain his freedom, the fallen Bishop of Rochester pointedly asked his visitors what hope there might be for men of lower station if they, the bishops, were so unmindful of their trust. "The fort is betraid," he said, "even of them that shoulde have defended yt." Confessing that he felt he had not long to live, he remarked to the bishops:

> I mind not (by the helpe of God) to trooble my conscience in pleasing the king this way, what soever become of me; but rather here to spend out the remnant of my ould days in praying to God for him.[17]

Saint John Fisher's fidelity to the allegiance he had sworn to the See of Peter years before was fully matched by that of the noble layman who was his fellow prisoner in the Tower. Repeated and futile efforts were made to win over Thomas More to the king's cause; in fact, at the close of the trial in

TO TRUTH

Westminster Hall which condemned him to death, the Lord Chancellor, Thomas Audeley, let it be known that if the prisoner would even then repent his obstinacy he might still, as he said, "taste the King's gracious pardon." It was the prisoner's last chance to save his life, but not the slightest pause was detected before this final temptation of More's earthly sojourn as he turned toward the judges to say:

> My Lords, I humbly thank you for your great good will. Howbeit, I make my petition unto God Almighty that it may please him to maintain me in this my honest mind, to the last hour that I shall live.[18]

Five days thereafter he went to his execution on Tower Hill in serene possession of a conscience disquieted by no forfeiture of a sacred trust.

To give one's life is, indeed, the ultimate

Thirteen

price that any man can pay for principle;
yet to Fisher and More this supreme sacrifice was never in serious question. An in-
spiring statement quoted several centuries
later of Ernst von Münchhausen, Minister
of Justice to King Frederick the Great of
Prussia, had seen its literal fulfillment in
Saints John Fisher and Thomas More, when
in response to the Prussian monarch's de-
mand that von Münchhausen change a law-
ful sentence, the latter had replied, "My
head indeed is at the disposal of Your Ma-
jesty, but not my conscience."[19] In this way
have Fisher and More and their kind come
to represent the embodiment of the advice
given by Polonius when he told his son:

> This above all: to thine own self be true
> And it must follow, as the night the day,
> Thou canst not then be false to any man.[20]

Nor does being true to one's self and to
one's conscience necessarily entail such ex-

treme alternatives as life or death; with most men the trial of personal integrity, and the value they set upon it, are tested within a simpler framework. So it was with the seventeenth-century Benedictine historian, Jean Mabillon, whose integrity encountered a challenge in his controversy with Jean-Armand de Rancé, Abbot of Notre Dame de la Trappe, over the requirements of the spiritual life. The point that probably aroused Mabillon more than any other was de Rancé's insinuation that in the course of their exchange of views the famed member of the Congregation of Saint Maur had written certain passages with diplomatic insincerity. "I may fall into error, like other men," Mabillon retorted. "I may even fall into inconsistency; but that I should write against my conviction – that, I trust, by the grace of God shall never happen to me."[21]

Fifteen

A COMMITMENT

To err is the lot of every man, and an impulse to conceal the error is a temptation which probably few if any men entirely escape. Only rarely, therefore, are the deep and shadowy recesses of man's interior life forced by his own merciless scrutiny to expose his defects in their true proportions. Yet it was a self scrutiny of that kind to which the young German Jesuit, Father Alfred Delp, submitted himself during the days that he languished in a Nazi prison awaiting his trial and execution which came in February, 1945. The exercise demands, one need hardly say, supreme courage, but Father Delp's situation was conducive to its success, and on New Year's Eve of 1944 he confided to his diary that the soul-searching had uncovered what he termed, "much vanity, arrogance and self-esteem; and in the past also a certain amount of dishonesty."

He confessed that he was made most keenly aware of it when the Nazi guards called him a liar while they proceeded to beat him in the hope that he would divulge the names of others of his circle who were hostile to the regime. The cleansing effect that such an ordeal could have on a man's soul was evident in the same diary entry which continued:

> I prayed hard, asking God why he permitted me to be so brutally handled and then I saw that there was in my nature a tendency to pretend and deceive.[22]

Before the transparent honesty of a mind such as this, one can only bow in homage, acknowledging that it is alone the very exceptional man who can sincerely say that he has never experienced a similar tendency in his interior life.

But when the great majority of men experience this 'tendency to pretend and deceive,' in other words, to betray the truth, and give way to the temptation, the action is normally confined within the limits of a private moral struggle about which the world knows nothing, the outcome of which does not involve others, and the effects of which are not sufficiently widespread or enduring to merit comment. But the higher men go in either Church or State the more inevitably does their rank embrace responsibility for leading others and for influencing their minds and course of action. For such men to succumb to a tendency to pretend and to deceive can mean inflicting irreparable harm, not alone on the individual's own character, but as well on the institution or community over which he has been set to rule. For as Cardinal Newman stated in viewing influence as a gift from God:

> He has given us a certain circle of persons, larger or smaller, who depend on us, whom

our words and our actions affect for good
or for evil, and ought to affect for good.
...All these are God's gifts to us, and they
are given us, not to be wasted but to be
used, to be turned to account...[for] we
shall have one day to answer for our use
of them.[23]

Both ecclesiastical and civil history offer
abundant evidence of the validity of this
judgment concerning the power of personal
influence; in fact, certain occurrences in history cannot be understood without a knowledge of the influences that brought them
about, unpleasant as that knowledge may at
times prove to be. Since, therefore, as Teilhard de Chardin has said, "... nothing is
comprehensible except through its history,"[24]
and since the Church is a prime concern of
all of us, let us illustrate the point through
several episodes that one encounters in her
long and eventful story.

First, let us speak of the case of Galileo,

Nineteen

of which considerable was heard during the sessions of Vatican Council II. The broad outline and principal facts of the matter are well known and need no restatement here. No one acquainted with the imperfect state of scientific knowledge in the early seventeenth century will take serious exception to the Holy Office's decision of 1616 – approved by Pope Paul V – which condemned Galileo for his espousal of the Copernican theory of the movement of the heavenly bodies; nor will they be unduly surprised at the same tribunal's second condenmation in 1633, in this instance with the approval of Pope Urban VIII. In fact, even so learned a contemporary as Saint Robert Bellarmine was held captive by the meager scientific data of the age, and in consequence believed Galileo to have been in error. Exception can, however, be taken to the churchmen's lack of theological perception in entering the realm of science on the basis of their quite incomplete knowledge. Rather than to have busied themselves with condemnations of the new scientific finds, it would have been more profitable to all concerned had these finds stimulated them to a deeper investigation into the meaning of Scripture and the extent to which it was capable of explaining scientific data. It was the violation of this approach that seeks first to understand the incontestable facts of science before they are condemned, that created the initial difficulty, a violation, needless to say, that can be as costly for the Church today as it was in Galileo's time. A remark made by Teilhard de Chardin in 1918 has pertinence here. He said:

> Those who are diffident, timid, under-developed, or narrow in their religion, I should like to remind that Christ required

for His body the full development of man,
and that mankind, therefore, has a duty
to the created world and to truth – namely,
the ineluctable duty of research.[25]

What, then, is to be said of those churchmen who, long after it had been proved
beyond peradventure that the earth went
around the sun, persisted in trying to sustain
the position of the Holy Office? What is a
curious mind to be told who inquires about
the fact that until 1757, a century and a
half after the original condemnation, any
work that stated the earth went around the
sun was *ipso facto* put on the Index of Pro-
hibited Books? How is one to answer the
charge that scientific knowledge was impeded
in Catholic circles, when until the middle
of the eighteenth century – and in some
cases far beyond that date – teachers in
many Catholic schools were not free to in-
struct students in the correct movement of

the heavenly bodies? What again is a con-
scientious scholar of the Church to say to
a learned non-Catholic colleague who may
remind him that as late as 1820 – more
than two centuries after Galileo's first condemnation – a book embodying the Copernican theory was refused an *imprimatur* at
Rome, and that only in 1822 was general
permission to print such books finally grant-
ed in the Eternal City?[26] There is but one
way to reply to questions of this kind,
whether they are posed by one outside the
Catholic fold or by one within, and that is
to state simply and without equivocation
that the churchmen who were responsible
for maintaining these policies in the face of
established scientific evidence to the contrary, were guilty of intellectual dishonesty.
Indeed, it is not easy to absolve them from
acting in bad faith, allowing that their ac-

tion was inspired by a mistaken notion of protecting the Church's interests. One may even wonder about the nature of their own doctrinal commitment, for as Maisie Ward once remarked:

> When one has no doubt that in fundamentals one is right and secure, one shrinks the less from complete candour. One does not tremble lest to face a new fact may mean to dissolve one's faith.[27]

The incalculable injury done to the reputation of the Catholic Church in learned circles by the Galileo case requires no emphasis. Coming as it did a century after the outbreak of the Protestant Revolt, this *cause célèbre* offered a classic example of the inflexibility of the siege mentality that had overtaken the vast majority of both Catholic and Protestant churchmen during the course of the sixteenth century. To admit that one had been wrong was to betray one's religious loyalty, and to give comfort to an enemy ever on the alert to discover a weak point in the adversary's armor. Thus was the mistake of the Roman Inquisition's commission of 1616 and 1633 permitted to harden with the passage of time, and the longer the attempt was made to defend the indefensible the more damaging were the results to all concerned.

It was not that the error of these seventeenth-century judges was not known among informed Catholics and deeply deplored, for it was. To cite a single instance, on January 3, 1870, Bishop Augustin Verot of Savannah, soon to be transferred to Saint Augustine, Florida, rose in Vatican Council I to urge the Church's obligation to treat natural science with the honesty and seriousness which were its due. He mentioned certain violations of this obligation, among which was that relating to Galileo, an example which, he confessed, he offered "with heaviness of heart," because the action of certain theologians in this case had occasioned what Verot described as "opprobrium upon religion, upon the Church, and upon this Holy See, which was always the patron of knowledge." He did not hesitate to brand the policy of Galileo's judges and their followers "a disaster for religion," and for that reason he implored that this page in the Church's history should be erased. Such an act, he stated, would "bring glory, great glory, to the Vatican Council, if due reparation is made to the memory of Galileo."[28] In spite of the justice of the bishop's petition and the cogency of his reasoning, however, the request was regarded as hardly more than an eccentric whim in those early days of 1870 when the issue of defining the pope's infallibility overshadowed all the conciliar deliberations.

Yet the ninety-six years that have intervened since Bishop Verot spoke at Rome have not brought complete ease to the Catholic conscience in regard to Galileo. His name was raised sympathetically more than once during Vatican Council II, among others by Cardinal Léon Joseph Suenens, Archbishop of Malines-Brussels, who on October 19, 1964, in urging the fathers to heed the aid that science might lend in solving the problems that relate to birth control, warned them, "The council should take care to avoid a new Galileo case. One such case in the history of the Church is quite enough!"[29] A week later Léon Arthur Elchinger, Coadjutor Bishop of Strasbourg, asked that the council vindicate Galileo's honor by a public confession of what he termed "the miserable and unjust condemnation" of the famous scientist.[30] This position received further support when there came to light about the same time the story of the scholarly efforts in Galileo's behalf of the late Monsignor Pio Paschini, professor of church history in the Lateran University. Early in the 1930's Paschini had completed an extensive and critical biography entitled 'The Life and Works of Galileo,' but he was denied an *imprimatur* on the score that its publication at the time might be used as a weapon against the pope's authority by the Fascists with whom Pius XI was then at serious odds. Meanwhile a generation passed and the accession of John XXIII brought to power one of Paschini's old friends, with the result that the approaching fourth centennial of Galileo's birth (1964) was used as an occasion for the long delayed publication of this objective study.[31]

As one reflects on this celebrated case it is difficult to escape the conclusion that an immeasurably improved relationship would have obtained between the Church and the scholarly world over the last 300 years, had the churchmen's faulty judgments of 1616 and 1633 – once the scientific evidence had been indisputably established – been promptly and openly admitted. What is, perhaps, equally disconcerting is the failure of cases like that of Galileo to teach a lesson. As late as 1927, for example, in discussing his differences with Marcellin Boule, his former professor, Teilhard de Chardin felt it necessary to state to a correspondent:

> ...it will be plain to you that as far as I am concerned I am not going to change my methods one iota. Before everything else comes research in its widest perspective – the service of truth.[32]

Twenty-nine

There does persist, indeed, a certain type of clerical mind that seems impervious to the conviction that in ecclesiastical as well as in profane affairs the merits of simple and straightforward speech far outweigh the value of concealment of awkward and unpleasant facts. This is not to deny that there is such a thing as a legitimate secret, or that in a particular situation the general interests may best be served by a policy of temporary or even lasting silence. But when it is a question of a truth to which men have a right – to say nothing of one of which they will inevitably become aware – attempts to hide it can only end in failure, and in that failure the Catholic name can only emerge tarnished and dishonored. Every educated person appreciates the difficulties that often attend the establishment of the truth, whether that be within or without the Church.

Thirty

For what has been said of the Holy Spirit's guidance of ecumenical councils can *mutatis mutandis* be said of His relationship to the Church in general, namely, that while He guarantees conciliar decisions to be free from error, He presupposes and demands that the most strenuous efforts be employed to arrive at the truths embodied in those decisions. The historian of the ecumenical councils summarized the point well when he wrote:

> Truth is reached in any community by means of an exchange of opinions, by arguments for and against, that is, by means of an intellectual struggle. At the councils, as in any other place where men contend with one another for the truth, fallen human nature exacts its toll: the former, that is the struggle, is ordained by God, the latter he permits.[33]

It would be a grave calumny on the moral rectitude of the Catholic clergy to suggest that a failure on the part of some to honor their commitment to truth gave warrant for suspicion concerning the integrity of all. Yet it would be equally foolhardy to deny that the casual manner in which certain churchmen have been known to treat the truth has not left that suspicion in many minds. In fact, it was the public expression of a misgiving of that kind that gave rise *per accidens* to one of the great spiritual autobiographies of all time. Informed students of the nineteenth-century Church are familiar with the chain of events that grew out of Charles Kingsley's review of Volumes VII and VIII of Froude's *History of England* in the January, 1864, issue of *Macmillan's Magazine*. Kingsley spoke caustically of what he described as "the dogma that the Pope of Rome had the power of creating right and wrong," and that not only truth and falsehood, but morality and immorality, had at one time depended on so simple a thing as a papal seal to a bit of parchment. He then went on to say:

> So, again, of the virtue of truth. Truth, for its own sake, had never been a virtue with the Roman clergy. Father Newman informs us that it need not, and on the whole ought not to be; that cunning is the weapon which Heaven has given to the saints wherewith to withstand the brute male force of the wicked world which marries and is given in marriage. Whether his notion be doctrinally correct or not, it is at least historically so.[34]

Rarely if ever in a long life filled with controversy was John Henry Newman so roused by a criticism as he was by this monstrous charge. He set himself at once to the task of answering Kingsley and late in April, 1864, there appeared the first of a series of pamphlets that were eventually to constitute the preface for Newman's *Apologia Pro Vita Sua* which was published at the end of that year. One need not tarry here to comment on the unforgettable manner in which Newman refuted the accusation of intellectual dishonesty in the elaborate account he gave of his religious opinions. All his life he manifested a special sensitivity on the point of personal honesty and truthfulness; in fact, Henry Tristram, who knew Newman's mind better than most men in the present century, maintained that two of the qualities that were most characteristic of the great Oratorian were his sense of the presence of God and his dislike of what he called "unreality." "He was at once repelled," said Father Tristram, "by the slightest pretense or insincerity or humbug, and it was a strong condemnation from him, if he said, so and so is so unreal."[35] Given this circumstance, one can better understand the force and fervor behind certain passages of the *Apologia Pro Vita Sua*.[36]

TO TRUTH

Betrayal of a commitment to truth can
take various forms, including the pretense
that one is in possession of knowledge that
is really not his. For, unfortunately, many
– including churchmen – have given no heed
to the lesson that history so clearly teaches,
and that William Stubbs, Anglican bishop-
historian of the last century, so well phrased
when he stated that as often

> the height of courage is to say I dare not,
> and the height of love is to say I will not,
> so the height of wisdom is to have learned
> to say, I do not know.[37]

There are men who seem to have no realiza-
tion of the confidence that can be inspired
by so simple a declaration as 'I do not
know,' or the equally shattered confidence
of discerning persons in one who gives the
appearance of having an answer to every
question. A candid admission of ignorance
or error, on the other hand, can actually be

Thirty-five

wonderfully influential in winning the confidence and support of others. A simple example of what I mean would be an editorial entitled "Our First Six Months" that appeared in *The Commonweal* in the spring of 1925. Noting the journal's birth six months before and reviewing some of the highlights of those early months, the editors frankly confessed:

> We have had many failures in living up to our own ideals. Many mistakes have been committed. It is only simple honesty to state the facts, but the greater fact remains that these six months have proved that there really is a place for a journal like *The Commonweal*, and that *The Commonweal* has found that place.[38]

The consensus of the present day but confirms the assertion of forty years ago about *The Commonweal* having found its place, and the success that has attended it in the intervening time has in no small measure been due to the intellectual honesty that has characterized its editorial policies. All of which, to be sure, is not to suggest that either editors or private individuals are called to give voice to every thought that crosses their minds. For fidelity to truth as used in the present context does not require a situation like that portrayed by Eugene O'Neill in *Strange Interlude*[39] where in fine print were disclosed the most secret ruminations of Nina Leeds, Charles Marsden, and the other characters about each other. The human condition allows each man to wear his invisible mask, for life would become unbearable were one compelled to remove that saving barrier behind which are concealed one's intimate views about others, and at times even about oneself! More important than the sacrifice of personal ease and comfort, however, the mask finds justification in one's inherent distrust of his own views about others and about himself, a distrust that is born of a man's awareness of how frequently he is mistaken and of how ill founded at times are his apparent convictions. Indeed, in this sense it can be an instrument by which one strengthens the charity that he should display toward all his fellowmen. Happily, then, the wearing of such a mask involves no violation of the principles of truthfulness and honesty in the sense in which we have been speaking here.

No discussion of the use or abuse of these qualities would be complete, however, without reference to what constituted in the judgment of many, the present century's most serious and sustained infraction of truth and honesty by a group of men presuming to speak in the Church's name. I refer to the movement that arose as an aftermath of Pope Pius X's condemnation of Modernism in 1907. Every well educated Catholic is aware that far from being a 'phantom heresy' – to use Félix Klein's appropriate term for the alleged heresy of Americanism[47] – Modernism was altogether real and gave genuine cause for alarm concerning the integrity of Catholic doctrine. But in the process of trying to rid the Church of the modernists and their errors, the gravest excesses were committed, and irreparable injury was done to Catholic scholarship, as well as to the personal reputations of numerous learned and respected figures both clerical and lay. In fact, if Pius X defined Modernism in his encyclical, *Pascendi dominici gregis* (September 8, 1907), as "a synthesis of all heresies,"[41] one is tempted to describe the integralist movement that followed as "a synthesis of all dishonesties."

Removed as we are by more than a half

century from the most aggressive and insolent manifestations of this evil spirit, it is not easy to recapture the atmosphere then prevalent in Catholic circles which was created by the dishonesty of means and depth of deception practised by the self-styled 'integral' Catholics. In response to the directives of central headquarters at Rome called the *Sodalitium Pianum* of which Monsignor Humberto Benigni was the moving spirit, a virtual reign of terror spread through the seminaries, colleges, and Catholic literary and social groups in the years leading up to World War I. Needless to say, original and scientific research and publication all but came to a standstill in this kind of situation where anyone who demurred from accepting the reactionary policies of the integralists, or from adopting their ultra-conservative interpretations of doctrinal and moral questions, became immediately a target of relentless abuse.

The list of the victims was a long and distinguished one and included Cardinals François Richard and Léon Amette of Paris and Désiré Mercier of ~~Louvain~~ *Malines*; educational administrators like Paulin Ladeuze, Rector of the Catholic University of Louvain, Pierre Batiffol who was hounded out of the rectorship of the Catholic Institute of Toulouse, and Henri-Marie Alfred Baudrillart, Rector of the Catholic Institute of Paris; celebrated scholars such as the Dominican friars, Marie Joseph LaGrange and Antonin D. Sertillanges, and the Jesuits, Jules Lebreton and Ferdinand Prat, as well as widely known and revered laymen of the stature of Georges Goyau, Léon Harmel, and Albert de Mun. These and many others were savagely attacked as modernists, liberals, or socialists, and their writings were combed for passages that might lend themselves to suspicion of doctrinal errancy. Accusations were repeated again and again in the face of the stoutest denials, and religious authorities were inundated with both public denunciations and anonymous delations in which the authors' words were torn from their context and interpolated or edited in such a way as to produce the desired effect.[42] Parenthetically, I am reminded here of a respected Sulpician scholar who told me about ten years ago of the injury done to his confrère, Auguste Brassac, Scripture professor at Paris, who, he said, had related to him how his (Brassac's) textbook had been brought into the classroom by a certain professor of Scripture in the Urban College of Propaganda, who, in turn, had read to the students Brassac's quotations of the rationalists' opinions on controverted points as the opinions of the author himself!

It would be easy to multiply instances of the mischief done by Benigni and his henchmen, but let one further example suffice. The Abbé Alfred Loisy was the leading modernist of the first years of the twentieth century, a former professor of Scripture at the Catholic Institute of Paris, who had been excommunicated in 1908. Some time thereafter a journal entitled *Rome*, which belonged to the Benigni chain of papers, fabricated a defence of Loisy which, it was stated, had been taken from the *Dublin Review*, which was then edited by Wilfrid Ward who had been marked for destruction by the integralists. "This sheer invention," said Ward's daughter, Maisie, "if Cardinal Rampolla [then Secretary of the Holy Office] had seen it, would have strengthened the impression he had received many years earlier that my father was a supporter of Loisy."[43]

Violence of this kind to the reputation of respected figures was bound to bring a reaction. A few feeble protests were raised from time to time by the advocates of honesty and fairplay; but they were drowned out by the din of lies, inventions, and calumnies that continued pretty much unabated until the pontificate had run its course. Only with the election of Cardinal Giacomo della Chiesa, Archbishop of Bologna, as Pope Benedict XV on September 3, 1914, did there dawn a substantial hope for the defeat of the integralist mentality and the prospect that truth and honesty might once more gain the ascendancy. Having disagreed with the *Sodalitium Pianum's* methods during his days in the Roman Curia, della Chiesa had not himself escaped attack before he left for the Archdiocese of Bologna in February, 1908. It was not surprising, therefore, that there should have manifested itself at the Vatican an almost immediate change of attitude toward Benigni and his followers. Renewed protests were now made against the integralists' policies and conduct, and in no instance were these expressed with more dignity and force than by Eudoxe-Irénée Mignot, Archbishop of Albi. In a famous and oft quoted letter to Cardinal Domenico Ferrata, Benedict XV's Secretary of State, in the second month of the new pontificate, Mignot fully acknowledged the gravity of the modernist heresy and the necessity for its being stamped out. He then came to the heart of the matter when he stated:

> In this doctrinal reaction, have not some of the underlings gone a good deal too far? Have they not sometimes given an impression of enmity to sincere and

A COMMITMENT

impartial research? There is no doubt of
this. And in consequence there is a real
wave of anger against authority among
scholars and thinkers everywhere. The
Church has lost some of the prestige which
was hers under Leo XIII. Within the
bosom of the Church, discouragement has
seized upon intellectual and social workers.
Denounced, spied upon, abused by the
papers of the occult power; held in suspicion by those who, deceived by false
reports, suspected the honesty of their in-
tentions – they found their work grown
very difficult. Many a man withdrew once
and for all from the lists who might have
won many a victory for the Christian
cause.

This sense of unrest has made itself
most unfortunately evident in many major
seminaries, in religious houses of study
and in university centres. Upon this, testi-
mony is unanimous: our young men have
lost the sacred passion for intellectual
labour, and it is very difficult for their
professors to stimulate it. After the enthusiasm – the often feverish enthusiasm
admittedly – for the study of apologetics,

exegesis, positive theology, philosophy and sociology, the students are now satisfied with a dull flat study, and theology of the handbook sort. Natural laziness has something to do with this, but many certainly think it the best way to assure their future and further their personal ambition. The perpetuation of this state of things will mean an inferior clergy, more concerned with the externals of worship than with the spiritual realities of interior religion – a clergy which will understand nothing of the intellectual and moral difficulties of the time, or of the movement of ideas, and the Church will be the loser. Such a clergy will stand motionless amidst a world on the march, a world whose light they ought to be. Neither their minds nor their hearts will be opened to those who are besieged by doubt, and so much in need of them.[44]

As it turned out, Cardinal Ferrata died rather suddenly on October 10 and Mignot's letter probably did not receive the consideration that it deserved. Yet three weeks later the point was taken up by the supreme authority in Benedict XV's first encyclical, *Ad beatissimi*, of November 1. Calling attention to the dissension that divided the Catholics, he urged that every effort be made to heal it, and to have them act in a united fashion. In that connection he warned:

> Again let no private person, either by the publication of books or journals, or by delivering discourses, publicly assume the position of a master in the Church....Concerning matters in which, since the Holy See has not pronounced judgment, saving faith and discipline, discussion may take place pro and contra, it is certainly lawful for everybody to say what he thinks and to uphold his opinion.

The Catholic who engaged in controversy was exhorted to avoid all intemperate language in his differences with others, to maintain his own views freely, yes, but modestly, and the pope then admonished:

> let him not imagine he is justified in cast-
> ing suspicion on the faith or discipline of
> those who hold a contrary opinion simply
> because they differ from him.[45]

Although the principal area of operations of Benigni's organization was western Europe, centering in cities like Paris, Vienna, and Brussels, their activities were widespread, and what might be called a suggestion of their spirit was manifest even in so distant a Church as that of the United States. Thus in the midst of the modernist scare the most learned American Catholic journal to date, the *New York Review*, was frightened out of existence in July, 1908.[46] Two years later Henry Poels, Dutch-born professor of Old Testament in the Catholic University of America, was compelled to resign because he would not subscribe to the Mosaic authorship of the Pentateuch. And a month before the final decision against

Poels, Cardinal Raphael Merry del Val,
Pius X's Secretary of State, set on foot an
investigation of Joseph Bruneau, S.S., professor of philosophy in Saint Mary's Seminary in Baltimore.[47] In neither the Poels
nor the Bruneau case was any evidence
found that linked these men to the modernists; nonetheless, their experience had a chil-
ling effect on Catholic seminary professors
throughout the land whose professional train-
ing and personal tastes might otherwise have
prompted them to engage in research and
publication beyond the purely routine level.

One would have imagined that an episode
such as we have been describing would have
made so profound an impression in ecclesiastical circles that the Church would have
been spared any resemblance of it through
the balance of the century. Unfortunately,
the integralist spirit was not exterminated

Fifty

by the decree of the Congregation of the Council of December, 1921, that officially put an end to the life of the *Sodalitium Pianum*.[48] Less than a generation later it had reappeared, and though the witchhunt tactics of the years after 1940 were never as brazen as in the days of Benigni, severe damage was done to a considerable number of people. For example, respected and devoted scholars like Henri de Lubac, S.J., and Yves Congar, O.P., were put under a cloud, and in 1961 two Jesuit professors of the Biblical Institute, Stanislaus Lyonnet and Maximilian Zerwick, were removed from their posts at the behest of the Holy Office. It is true that they were restored in 1964, but that did not change the unfortunate manner of their dismissal three years before. Here in the United States the distinguished Woodstock Jesuit, John Courtney Murray, was silenced for the better part of a decade on the subject of his special competence, the theology of religious freedom. Furthermore, the Holy Office's *monitum* of 1956 against the writings of A. Terruwe involved this lady psychiatrist of the Catholic University of Nijmegen in a long and painful ordeal that was not satisfactorily terminated until April of 1965 when an official announcement of her orthodoxy was issued by the office of the Cardinal Archbishop of Utrecht. In this case, incidentally, the Holy Office for the first time publicly withdrew a *monitum* that it had issued, which prompted a recent writer to express the hope that it "may be an indication that curial reform is beginning."[49]

True, the sequel to the Terruwe case would seem to offer a happy omen, as did the presence of Father Murray as a conciliar *peritus* in the aula of Saint Peter's Basilica on the morning of September 21, 1965, where he witnessed the triumph of his long and arduous struggle in the acceptance of the schema of the Secretariat for the Promotion of Christian Unity on religious freedom, largely his composition, by a vote of 1997 to 224. Yet the history of the type of thing we have been tracing here is not reassuring; it rather suggests that the price to be paid for truth, honesty, and freedom of inquiry within the Church is often about the same as it is without, namely, eternal vigilance. This does not imply that all the conservative churchmen who have opposed what might be called the progressive point of view were men devoid of respect for truth and honesty. On the contrary, many of them have been altogether sincere in their opposition. But it is to state that there has also been a cer-

tain element whose conduct would not pre-
suppose high personal integrity, adversaries
who have frequently demonstrated remarkable skill and resourcefulness. And to these
there can be paid the compliment that they
rarely succumb to the weakness of recog-
nizing when they have been defeated.

To remain silent, however, in all of this
about the noble defense that open and honest
inquiry has found within the Church might
well leave a quite false impression. Speaking
solely of the contemporary scene and without reference to the more remote past, mag-
nificient support of the principles of truth
and honesty were repeatedly voiced in Vatican Council II. Permit me to mention several
that became part of the record of that
historic gathering. On October 6, 1964, Basil
Christopher Butler, O.S.B., Abbot of Down-
side Abbey, addressed the council during

the debate on revelation. Much had been accomplished, he said, in driving out the spirit of excessive fear and anxiety which militated against the truth during what the abbot described as "this almost miraculous council." Since the aim of the Church's scholars was to reach what he termed "the full, objective, and real truth of the gospel tradition," there should be no misgiving. To be sure, some might turn liberty into license and just as surely some errors would be made; but these were risks that had to be taken for the greater good in a field in which, said Abbot Butler, "trial and error are the road to truth." The heart of the learned Benedictine's message was contained in these words:

> What we want is not the childish comfort which comes from averting our gaze from the truth, but a truly critical scholarship

Fifty-five

which will enable us to enter into a 'dia-
logue' with non-Catholic scholars.[50]

Six weeks later Paul Emile Legér, Cardinal
Archbishop of Montreal, returned to the
point of the freedom necessary for research
in the sacred sciences. Alluding to the complicated nature of our society, he spoke of
the need that the Church has for the very
best that her creative minds could furnish,
and for that kind of service scholars must
have freedom to pursue their studies. "If
this liberty is not perfectly assured," said
Cardinal Legér, "it would be possible that
irprearable damage would follow for the
Church."[51]

One of the most forceful and effective
expressions of this point of view came in
the council's fourth and final session and
was voiced by the recently appointed Archbishop of Turin, Michele Pellegrino, who

brought to the discussion a particular sensitivity and knowledge from his years as a professor of history in the University of Turin. Speaking on October 1, 1965, he acknowledged the right and duty of ecclesiastical authority to watch closely over developments in the sacred sciences, but this vigilance should be exercised, he said, "with due reverence for human dignity, which includes freedom of inquiry." The supreme authority was thanked for having averted the calamity of Modernism, but he then declared, in words reminiscent of those of Archbishop Mignot in 1914, that no one would dare to assert that in the repression of the modernist heresy the rights and dignity of churchmen had always been respected. Nor was this solely a phenomenon of the past, since a few years before, he said, "I found a religious living in involuntary exile for having expressed opinions which today we read in papal and conciliar documents;" and this was not, he added, a unique case. In conclusion Archbishop Pellegrino made clear the connection between truth and honesty and the freedom of inquiry necessary in intellectual pursuits when he said:

> If each one knows that he is permitted to express his opinion with wholesome freedom, he will act with the straightforwardness and sincerity that should shine in the Church; otherwise the abominable plague of dishonesty and hypocrisy can hardly be avoided.[52]

For the Archbishop of Turın to speak in terms of an "abominable plague of dishonesty and hypocrisy" was not to indulge in literary license; rather it was a candid admission of the characteristics that at times have dominated the policies and conduct of some Catholics. Admittedly, when these qualities are found in those who wield authority, it is often exceedingly difficult for the individual to do otherwise than to conform. Yet the highest type of obedience, as Father Josef Ratzinger has said, remains "forthright truthfulness," for what the Church needs today and has always needed, in the words of the ~~Innsbruck~~ *Tübingen* theologian

> are not adulators to extol the status quo, but men whose humility and obedience are no less than their passion for truth; men who brave every misunderstanding and attack as they bear witness; men who, in a word, love the Church more than ease and the unruffled course of their personal destiny.[53]

And of such men the Church of our time has not, indeed, been lacking. Let me mention only two whose names are familiar. It has been the transparent honesty of Cardinal Augustin Bea that has won him an unparalleled esteem in religious circles outside the Catholic fold, the kind of esteem that

A COMMITMENT

was reflected in an editorial of the *Christian Century* in the spring of 1965. Commenting on his denial of revisions in the conciliar schema on the Jews, the editorial stated:

> When Augustin Cardinal Bea speaks, most ecumenically minded Protestants listen. They may not agree with or gullibly accept what he says, but they listen. Because of what Cardinal Bea is personally and because of the unquestionable sincerity of his devotion to Christian unity, he gets a respectful Protestant ear. If what the cardinal says at one time needs modification later, that can be credited to his human limitations. It should not be credited to duplicity.[54]

Confidence of the type implied in that editorial represents a respect of a very high order for the Church, and it could have been inspired only by the utterly unequivocal conduct that has marked the career of the President of the Secretariat for the Promotion of Christian Unity.

Sixty

The second example is a churchman whose heroic and open fidelity to the truth has not only rendered an abiding service to the Church, but a man whose witness to that truth entailed the sacrifice of fifteen of the best years of his life in Nazi and Communist prisons, namely, Joseph Beran, Cardinal Archbishop of Prague. That was why the first applause heard in the aula of Saint Peter's on that historic morning of September 21, 1965, from the more than 2,000 fathers of Vatican Council II came as the Cardinal of Prague mounted the podium. Addressing himself to the schema on religious freedom, he spoke with great feeling about the unhappy effects that follow from a denial of such freedom, and in this connection he said:

> Everywhere, and always, the violation of liberty of conscience gives birth to hypocrisy in many people. And, perhaps,

one can say that hypocrisy in the profession of the faith is more harmful to the Church than the hypocrisy of hiding the faith, which anyway is more common in our times.

So, in my country, the Catholic Church at this time seems to be suffering expiation for defects and sins committed in times gone by in her name against religious liberty, such as in the fifteenth century the burning of the priest John Huss and during the seventeenth century the forced re-conversion of a great part of the Czech people to the Catholic faith, under the rule 'whoever's territory it is, that also is his religion.'[55]

It would be easy for those whose lives are spent mainly in academic pursuits to associate problems relating to truth, honesty, and free inquiry within a narrow academic framework. Unquestionably, these problems have on occasion been all too real for the scholar and the student; but the evils that arise from Catholics' failure to honor their commitment to truth are by no means confined to academic communities, as Cardinal Beran illustrated in the conciliar intervention just quoted. Actually, they exist on a broad front and appear in a variety of aspects of Catholic endeavor, as perceptive laymen like John Cogley and Daniel Callahan have been at pains to demonstrate.[56] The point might be exemplified in a number of different ways, for instance, in the field of American municipal politics where frequently Catholics have been confronted by a crisis in honesty from which some have emerged with honor neither to themselves nor to their Church. This has been a painfully apparent fact in the histories of cities like Boston, Chicago, Kansas City, New York, and San Francisco, not to mention others. And this failure at the municipal level has, perhaps, been all the more conspicuous because of the honorable manner in which most Catholics have discharged their political duties on the national level since the first of their number won cabinet rank in July, 1831, when President Jackson chose Roger Brooke Taney of Maryland to be Attorney General of the United States.

If there are certain attitudes and actions of the young people of this generation that I have found puzzling, there is one point in their thinking with which I am in complete sympathy, and that is their search for reality and their insistence that no counterfeits be accepted in its place. The focus of this generation's moral critique, according to Roger W. Heyns, Chancellor of the University of California at Berkeley, is hypocrisy. "That is why its angry negations," says Dr. Heyns, "like those of the prophets—are stronger than its affirmations. That is why it is surer of what is wrong with where we are as a society, than of where we ought to go. Prophets are not redeemers."[57]

I should like to think that this characteristic of contemporary youth is a manifestation of their commitment to truth. If that be the case, it is a perfectly valid form, surely, and if pursued in a positive and rational manner can help to lead them safely and profitably through society's increasingly complicated and bewildering labyrinth. Unless I have misread the late Pope John, it was an attitude somewhat akin to this that he intended to inculate when he told a group of Italian seminarians in the spring of 1961:

> I want to recommend to you a clear, cool view of present reality; a reality which is full of anxieties just as it has always been....Today in the seminary you are not preparing yourselves for service in an ideal chimerical world; if you have been thinking this you are in for bitter

disillusionment. Make no mistake about
it. The true priest of the Lord does not
live by nourishing dreams of unattainable
earthly happiness, much less of comfort
and well-being. Nor does he waste time
lamenting past happy ages, which never
were in reality. It is the same today as
it was yesterday and always will be: we
shall have to fight, and to remain solid
in faith and charity.[58]

Developments within the Church in the
brief span of time since Angelo Roncalli
ascended the throne of Peter in October,
1958, have prompted some writers to speak
of a "Johannine revolution"[59] among the
people of God. If the term be warranted,
the inspiration behind the change may be
said to have been drawn in no small degree
from Pope John's passion for reality and
his constant concern that men should reverence truth and honesty in every phase of
human endeavor. It is not the business of

the historian to play the role of the prophet, to assess the causes of events without evidence, or to dwell on what might have been; it is his business simply to say what was, and to interpret that for others to the best of his ability. I doubt, however, that an historian of contemporary Catholicism will be seriously challenged or considered rash if he assigns John XXIII's crusade for truth as a major factor in bringing about the new psychology that pervades ecclesiastical affairs. Less than a generation ago, for example, it would be difficult to think of an official of the Congregation of Rites publicly deploring the use for altar stones of what he termed "so-called 'holy bodies' taken from the catacombs." Yet in a recent issue of *Notitiae*, the journal of the post-conciliar liturgical commission, that view was expressed by Amato Pietro Frutaz, the congregation's under-secretary for beatification and canonization causes. In some cases, said Monsignor Frutaz, the relics used in altars have been "neither bodies of martyrs nor of other saints recognized as such;" and in the light of this dishonest practice he wisely suggested that the requirement that altar stones contain relics should be abolished and that they merely be consecrated with holy chrism.[60]

If there is any area of the Church's life where the utmost effort should constantly be employed to assure respect for truth and honesty, it is in all that pertains to liturgical worship and to religious devotions, both public and private. Yet it is precisely here that some of the most patent frauds have been perpetuated. Ours is not a generation that suffers saccharine piety gladly and, it may be added, the mounting numbers of well educated Catholics feel more and more a distaste for such. That is why those acquainted with the splendid work done by the French Benedictines of the Congregation of Saint Maur and the Jesuits of the Bollandist Society in Belgium in rescuing the lives of the saints from the jungle of legend, myth, and falsehood that have too often entangled them will ever hold these learned religious in grateful memory. For the same reason one is thankful to Herbert Thurston, S.J., and Donald Attwater whose meticulous and scholarly labors placed Alban Butler's multi-volumed work, *The Lives of the Saints*,[61] on a solid factual basis that has contributed far more ultimate edification than had the uncritical and unreal biographies of so many holy men and women.

The task of the Maurists and Bollandists has at times been deeply painful and unpleasant when fidelity to truth and to professional integrity have compelled the exposure of deliberate falsehoods by ecclesiastics of an earlier day. One of the most notorious instances of this kind involved two members of the religious order founded by Saint John of Matha who were guilty centuries after the latter's death of fabricating tales about him. As Thurston and Attwater stated:

> They knew practically nothing of the history of their founder, and in the fifteenth and sixteenth centuries, feeling handicapped by this ignorance and spurred on by rivalry with the Mercedarians, Hospitallers and others, certain writers of the order deliberately compiled a fictitious record which they professed to base on documentary evidence. This procedure is the more regrettable because it did not take place in the dark ages but in comparatively modern times. It appears plain that some few individuals, under pretext

of edification, did not scruple to invent a
chronicle of glorious achievements, studded
at every turn with supposed miracles and
supernatural revelations, and to palm all
this off upon their unsuspecting readers
as a history of the beginnings of the order.
Painful as the fact may be, it deserves to
be remembered, for it forms the justification of the severely critical and sceptical
attitude of the scientific hagiographers of
the present day.[62]

Nor were these fraudulent biographies an
isolated case, for other instances of this type
could be mentioned of saints who have not
benefitted to the same degree as John of
Matha from the critical and constructive
eye of a Bollandist historian. For example,
nearly sixty years passed after the publication of the autobiography of Saint Thérèse
of Lisieux edited by her sister, Mother Agnes
of Jesus, before the original and true text
of that remarkable spiritual memoir revealed

the liberties that had been taken in the version given to the world in 1898.[63]

In fact, the false stories circulated about saints are abnormally prevalent, some of which seem to defy suppression even after clear proof of their falsity has been established beyond doubt. In many instances a legend has become embedded in the religious folklore of a local region, for example, the shrine of the Magi in the cathedral of Cologne, as well as the tale of Saint Ursula and the virgin martyrs in the same region, the latter having been recommended for suppression over two centuries ago by a commission of Pope Benedict XIV.[64] In the same category are the alleged tombs of Mary Magdalen and Lazarus near Marseilles in France, a tale first heard in the eleventh century, and which was long ago demolished by the distinguished church historian, Monsignor Louis

Duchesne. And even though this myth lives on, Thurston and Attwater were right when they maintained that in spite of what they described as "the defence of those piously concerned on behalf of the local belief," it is indisputably true, as they said, "that the whole story is a fabrication."[65] It will be recalled, too, that as recently as 1961 the Congregation of Rites saw fit to strike the name of Philomena[66] from the list of the saints and to delete from the missal the Mass of George because of his doubtful authenticity.

Yet how many people are still departing from Catholic centers of worship, especially from pilgrim and shrine churches both here and abroad, repelled by the patently false claims made for certain objects, as well as by the dishonest practices that have grown up around them? I recall a visit made in

A COMMITMENT

May, 1950, to the shrine of Saint Anthony at Padua where the group with whom I was traveling was taken behind the main altar to a large reliquary. As it happened, it was an American Conventual Franciscan who was deputed that particular day to display the various exhibits. Among those taken from their high place above the floor of the church, I confess that I found one of an obviously spurious character particularly offensive, namely, a small vial which, we were told by the friar, contained some of the milk of the Blessed Mother! In another context a widely known devotion to which a false note is often attached is the novena held each year in anticipation of the feast of Saint Anne on July 26. Needless to say, no Catholic questions that our Lady had a mother, and that to this privileged soul who bore the Mother of the Son of God into this world, there is owed love and reverence. But this fact in no way justifies her alleged relics being brought forth for people's veneration, when as well informed persons know, not even the name 'Anne' was mentioned anywhere before the middle of the second century.

In all of this the commitment to truth that men have a right to expect from those who speak in the name of Christ and who are privileged to exercise His ministry is, it seems to me, gravely violated. The natural human tendency to superstition, or even to religious fanaticism in one form or another, is a phenomenon that is as old as the human race, and through every age thoughtful religious leaders have taken extraordinary precautions to keep them within bounds. Practices such as we have been describing, however, foster these unhappy tendencies and contribute to the stultification, not the progress, of true religious values.

This is a particularly critical moment in time when, as has been said, those of the rising generation have put a special premium on authenticity, on reality, and on all that is opposed to hypocrisy. The struggle in which the Church is now engaged to make herself relevant to men – exemplified in Vatican Council II's schema on the Church and the Modern World – will, therefore, be like Macbeth's tale "told by an idiot, full of sound and fury, signifying nothing,"[67] unless her teaching, her intellectual apostolate, her liturgy and worship, yes, and the lives of her sons and daughters, bear a note of authenticity and carry the credentials of truth and honesty. If these be lacking, then, the Church's voice will be mute in the academic and learned circles where the ideas that will shape tomorrow's world are being born; in national politics and international affairs where vital issues like civil rights and nuclear warfare clamor for decision; and in the marketplace where the Church aspires to have her doctrine of social justice temper the transactions by which men earn their livelihood and accumulate their fortunes. Some Catholics may be tempted to think a commitment to truth with all that that implies beyond their capacity to fulfill and that, therefore, they may as well not even try. This would be a fatal error that would undermine and nullify their every action. Rather it is incumbent on each individual, whatever be his or her walk in life, to strive incessantly to relate their thinking, speaking, and acting to what is true and real. And in the execution of this grave responsibility on

every Christian conscience, one could scarce-
ly do better than to make one's own Newman's words:

> Let us aim at meaning what we say, and
> saying what we mean; let us aim at know-
> ing when we understand a truth, and
> when we do not. When we do not, let us
> take it on faith, and let us profess to do
> so. Let us receive the truth in reverence,
> and pray God to give us a good will, and
> divine light, and spiritual strength, that
> it may bear fruit within us.[68]

NOTES

Monsignor Ellis is professor of church history in the University of San Francisco. He wishes to express his sincere gratitude to his friend, the Reverend Raymond G. Decker, professor of theology in the San Francisco College for Women, for a critical reading of the manuscript which led, in turn, to a number of helpful suggestions and pertinent references which he generaously contributed.

1. "Pope John XXIII, In Memoriam," *The Christian Century*, LXXX (June 26, 1963), 823.

2. *The Encyclicals and Other Messages of John XXIII*, edited by the staff of The Pope Speaks Magazine (Washington: TPS Press, 1964), p. 29.

3. "Truth in Our Time," *The Tablet* (London), CCXIV (December 31, 1960), 1213.

4. *John XXIII, Pope Paul on His Predecessor and a Documentation by the Editors of 'Herder Correspondence'* (New York: Herder and Herder, 1964), pp. 112-113.

5. *Exodus*, XX, 14-16.

6. *Matthew*, XIV, 1-12.

7. *John*, III, 28-30.

8. *Matthew*, XI, 11.

9. *Mark*, X, 35-40.

A COMMITMENT

10. *John*, VIII, 3-11.

11. *Luke*, XXII, 61.

12. *Matthew*, XXIII, 5-7.

13. *Ibid.*, XXIII, 27-28.

14. *Ibid.*, XXIV, 51.

15. Giorgio del Vecchio, "Paolo and Francesca. Justice, Love and Sin in Dante," *Wiseman Review*, No. 487 (Summer, 1961), 160.

16. David Knowles, *The Historian and Character and Other Essays* (Cambridge: At the University Press, 1963), p. 14. The lecture in question was delivered on November 17, 1954.

17. François Van Ostroy, S.J. (Ed.), "Vie du Bien-heureux Martyr Jean Fisher, Cardinal, Evêque de Rochester (+1535)," *Annalecta Bollandiana*, XII (1893), 159.

18. R. W. Chambers, *Thomas More* (New York: Harcourt Brace and Company Inc., 1935), p. 335.

19. *English Catholic Newsletter*, No. 105 (November 15, 1941).

20. *Hamlet*, Act I, Scene 3. Whether Polonius' speech be interpreted as a Shakespearean exercise in satire, as some scholars hold, the point in this instance was a sound bit of advice.

21. M. D. Knowles, "Jean Mabillon." *Journal of Eccle-*

siastical History, X (October, 1959), 169, quoting L. Delisle, "Dom Jean Mabillon. Sa Probité d'historie," *Mélanges Archives de la France monastique* (Paris and Liguge: Abbaye de Saint–Martin, 1908), pp. 93-103.

22. *The Prison Meditations of Father Alfred Delp*. With an introduction by Thomas Merton (New York: Herder and Herder, 1963), p. 12.

23. *Faith and Prejudice and Other Unpublished Sermons of Cardinal Newman* edited by the Birmingham Oratory (New York: Sheed and Ward, 1956), pp. 101-102. The title of this sermon, preached on July 31, 1870, was "Stewards and Also Sons of God."

24. Pierre Teilhard de Chardin, *The Future of Man*. Translated from the French by Norman Denny (New York: Harper & Row, 1964), p. 12.

25. Pierre Teilhard de Chardin, "Le Pretre," an unpublished manuscript of 1918, Claude Cuénot, *Teilhard de Chardin, A Biographical Study*. Translated by Vincent Colimore and edited by Rene Hague. (London: Burns Oates, 1965), p. 40.

26. Walter J. Ong, S.J., *American Catholic Crossroads* (New York: Macmillan Company, 1959), p. 108. For a recent brief treatment of the Galileo case, see James Brodrick, S.J., *Galileo and the Roman Inquisition* (London: Catholic Truth Society, 1963).

27. Maisie Ward, *The Wilfrid Wards and the Transition* (New York: Sheed & Ward, Inc., 1934), p. 35.

28. Michael V. Gannon, *Rebel Bishop, The Life and*

A COMMITMENT

Era of Augustin Verot (Milwaukee: Bruce Publishing Company, 1964), p. 204.

29. *The Monitor* (San Francisco), November 5, 1964, p. 2.

30. San Francisco *Examiner*, November 5, 1964, p. 68.

31. *The Monitor* (San Francisco), December 3, 1964, p. 8.

32. Teilhard de Chardin to an unnamed correspondent, February 27, 1927, Cuénot, *op. cit.*, p. 81.

33. Hubert Jedin, *Ecumenical Councils of the Catholic Church. An Historical Outline* (New York: Herder and Herder, 1960), p. 234.

34. "Mr Kingsley and Dr. Newman: A Correspondence on the Question Whether Dr. Newman Teaches that Truth is No Virtue?" Appendix I, Charles Frederick Harrold (Ed.), John Henry Cardinal Newman, *Apologia Pro Vita Sua* (New York: Longmans, Green and Company, 1947), p. 358.

35. Henry Tristram (Ed.), *Meditations and Devotions by John Henry Newman* (New York: Longmans, Green and Company, 1953), pp. xiii-xiv.

36. A more recent example of a similar charge occurred in Edmund Wilson's memoirs, *A Piece of My Mind. Reflections at Sixty* (New York: Farrar, Straus and Cudahy, 1956). Wilson accused the editors of *America* of carrying a highly critical article about his book on the Dead Sea Scrolls by John J. Dougherty in the same

issue with a friendly review of the volume by Frederick
L. Moriarty, S.J. Wilson 'imagined' that the Dougherty
article was deliberately published in the same issue to
offset the Moriarty review (p. 16), and he concluded:

> The Catholic, then, does not have to be honest
> in the sense in which the term is ordinarily
> used—any more than the Communist does. He
> deals with the fool according to his folly; he
> defends the high faith he professes by bringing
> it down within the range of the low; he is free
> to think whatever he pleases if he makes a
> routine submission (p. 17).

37. *Seventeen Lectures on the Study of Mediaeval and
Modern History* (Oxford: At the Clarendon Press, 1886),
p. 95. The lecture in question was delivered in May,
1877.

38. *The Commonweal*, I (April, 1925), 670.

39. (New York: Boni & Liveright, 1928).

40. *Americanism: A Phantom Heresy* (Atchison, Kansas: Aquin Book Shop, 1951).

41. *Encyclical Letter of . . . . Pius X . . . . on the Teach-
ings of the Modernists*. Authorized translation (Dublin:
Browne & Nolan, Ltd., 1907), p. 44.

42. Among recent accounts of this group the following
are worthy of mention: " 'La Sapinière' ou brève histoire de l'organisation intégriste," by Louis Davallon
[a pseudonym], *Chronique Sociale de France*, Cahier 3
(May 15, 1955), 241-261; Robert A. Graham, S.J.,

A COMMITMENT

"Ends and Means in Controversy," *America*, LXXXV (April 14, 1956), 54-56, based for the most part on Davallon; the chapter, "Modernists and Integralists," in Walter H. Peters, *The Life of Benedict XV* (Milwaukee: Bruce Publishing Company, 1959), pp. 42-53; Gerald J. O'Brien, S.J., "Anti-Modernism: The Integralist Campaign," *Continuum*, III (Summer, 1965), 187-200.

43. Maisie Ward, *Insurrection versus Resurrection* (New York: Sheed & Ward, 1937), p. 325.

44. Mignot to Ferrata, October, 1914, Nicolas Fontaine, *Saint Siège, Action française et Catholiques intégraux. Histoire critique avec documents* (Paris: Librairie Universitaire. J. Gamber, 1928), p. 133. It has been said that Fontaine was a pseudonym for M. Canet, an official of the Quay d'Orsay who dealt with religious groups. See O'Brien, *loc. cit.*, p. 195, n. 34.

45. "First Encyclical of Benedict XV," *Catholic Mind*, XII (December 22, 1914), 745-746.

46. E. Harold Smith, "Recollections of the Aftermath," *Continuum*, III (Summer, 1965), 234-235.

47. John Tracy Ellis, *The Life of James Cardinal Gibbons, Archbishop of Baltimore, 1834-1921* (Milwaukee: Bruce Publishing Company, 1952), II, 171-182; 475-476.
48. Davallon, *loc. cit.*, p. 256.

49. "Holy Office Rehabilitates Psychiatrist," *Herder Correspondence*, II (September-October, 1965), 290.

50. "Divine Revelation. Abbot Butler's Council

Speech," *The Tablet*, CCXVIII (October 10, 1964), 1135.

51. Mimeographed summary of interventions, "l'Education Chrètienne. Schema: les Ecoles catholiques," sent to the writer through the kindness of Edward M. Gaffney of the North American College, Rome.

52. "Council Digest Prepared for the Council Fathers of the United States, 140th General Congregation, October 1, 1965," p. 5, furnished to the writer through the kindness of the Reverend Robert Trisco., associate professor of church history in the Catholic University of America.

53. Josef Ratzinger, ⚞, "Free Expression and Obedience in the Church," *The Church. Readings in Theology*, edited by Albert La Pierre *et al.*, at the Canisianum, Innsbruck. (New York: P. J. Kenedy & Sons, 1963), p. 212.

54. *The Christian Century*, LXXXII (May 19, 1965), 637.

55. "On Religious Liberty, Intervention of Joseph Cardinal Beran, Vatican Council II, September 21, 1965." The writer is grateful to the Reverend Robert Roh for a copy of the English translation of this document. The schema on religious freedom was finally approved by the council fathers on November 19, 1965, by a vote of 1,954 to 249. San Francisco *Chronicle*, November 20, 1965, p. 8.

56. John Cogley, "Honesty vs Loyalty Oaths," *The Commonweal*, LXXX (May 11, 1964), 249-251. Daniel

A COMMITMENT

Callahan, "The Quest for Honesty," *The Commonweal* LXXXI (April 24, 1964), 137-140, and *Honesty in the Church* (New York: Charles Scribner's Sons, 1965).

57. San Francisco *Chronicle*, November 13, 1965, p. 7. The statement was made in an address to the Commonwealth Club of San Francisco the previous day.

58. *The Tablet* (London), CCXVI (April 15, 1961), 369. On the occasion of the fourth centenary of the establishment of seminaries by the Council of Trent, Pope Paul VI issued an apostolic letter, *Summi Dei verbum*, November 4, 1963, in which he said *inter alia*:

> Moreover, in his dealings with others the man who wants to bear witness before the world— with Christ and for Christ— to see that truth which brings freedom must be trained in the virtue of truth in word and action, and so must cultivate sincerity, loyalty, integrity, fidelity. [*Summi Dei verbum*....(Washington: N.C.W.C. News Service. 1963), p. 13.]

59. For example, E.E.Y. Hales, *Pope John and His Revolution* (Garden City: Doubleday and Company, Inc. 1965).

60. *The Register* (Denver), October 31, 1965, p. 5, which gave a summary of the Frutax article from the September-October issue of *Notitiae*.

61. *Butler's Lives of the Saints*. Complete Edition. Edited, Revised and Supplemented by Herbert Thurston, S.J., and Donald Attwater. 4 volumes. (New York: P. J. Kenedy & Sons. 1956).

62. *Ibid.*, I, 277. G. G. Coulton cited a somewhat similar instance in speaking of Andreas Agnellus (805-c.846)
who wrote a history of the Bishops of Ravenna. Of that
work Coulton stated:

> Somewhere about A.D. 850 Agnellus, Bishop
> of Ravenna, undertook to write a complete
> series of lives of his predecessors in that see. He
> was for his own time, a remarkable scholar:
> yet here is his description of his historical
> methods. (Where I have not found any history
> of any of these bishops, and have not been able
> by conversation with aged men, or inspection
> of the monuments, or from any other authen-
> tic source, to obtain information concerning
> them, in such a case, in order that there might
> not be a break in the series, I have composed
> the life myself, with the help of God and the
> prayers of the brethren.) [*Medieval Panorama*
> (New York: Macmillan Company, 1938),
> p. 439].

63. *Autobiography of St. Thérèse of Lisieux.* Translated
by Ronald Knox from *L'Histoire d'une ame.* (New York:
P. J. Kenedy & Sons, 1958). The French original was
published in 1957.

64. *Butler's Lives of the Saints*, IV, 165.

65. *Ibid.*, III, 163.

66. *Acta Apostolicae Sedis*, LIII (March 29, 1961), 174.

67. Macbeth, V., v.

A COMMITMENT

68. "Words," preached on June 2, 1839, Vincent Ferrer Blehl, S.J. (Ed.), *Cardinal Newman's Best Plain Sermons* (New York: Herder and Herder, 1964), p. 83.

INDEX

Index